ULTIMATE COLLECTION OF

INSPIRATIONAL QUOTES

FUEL YOUR JOURNEY TO SUCCESS, GREATNESS AND POWER

PROF. JOSEPH CANISIUS NDUNGURU

BlueRose ONE.com DIY
Stories Matter
NewDelhi • London

BLUEROSE PUBLISHERS
India | U.K.

BlueRose ONE.com DIY
Stories Matter
NewDelhi • London

For permissions requests or inquiries regarding this publication, please contact:

BLUEROSE PUBLISHERS
www.BlueRoseONE.com
info@bluerosepublishers.com
+91 8882 898 898
+4407342408967

ISBN: 978-93-7139-772-8

First Edition: August 2025

ABSTRACT

This book is a curated collection of powerful quotes that fuel your journey to success, greatness, and inner power. It is designed for dreamers, doers, and difference-makers who seek to ignite their passion and drive through the wisdom of history's greatest thinkers. The quotes are thoughtfully organized into categories that address various facets of human experience, offering guidance and inspiration across different life domains.

1. Personal Growth & Success Quotes:

These quotes are a source of motivation, encouraging readers to overcome challenges, persist through adversity, and never give up on their dreams. They emphasize the importance of hard work, resilience, and embracing failure as a steppingstone to success.

2. Wisdom & Reflection Quotes:

This section invites introspection and thoughtfulness, offering deep insights into life, philosophy, and personal development. The words of sages and philosophers challenge readers to question their assumptions and explore the deeper meaning of existence.

3. Love & Relationships Quotes:

Love, compassion, and empathy are explored in this category. These quotes remind us of the value of human connection, the power of kindness, and the strength that comes from love. They inspire readers to nurture relationships and embrace the transformative power of love.

4. Leadership & Motivation Quotes:

The leadership section focuses on the qualities that make great leaders, including vision, courage, and the ability to inspire others. These quotes offer practical wisdom for those seeking to lead with integrity and build a path of influence that empowers others.

5. Justice & Equality Quotes:

This section shines a light on fairness, justice, and the fight for equality. It includes quotes that advocate for social justice, human rights, and the importance of standing up for what is right, inspiring readers to act and make a positive difference in the world.

This abstract offers a glimpse into the diverse and thought-provoking content that fills the pages of this motivational eBook. Each quote serves as a catalyst for change, urging readers to think deeply, act, and strive for greatness in every aspect of their lives.

"We cannot solve problems with the kind of thinking we employed when we came up with them." –Albert Einstein

*****

"Learn as if you will live forever, live like you will die tomorrow." –Mahatma Gandhi

*****

"Stay away from those people who try to disparage your ambitions. Small minds will always do that, but great minds will give you a feeling that you can become great too." –Mark Twain

*****

"When you give joy to other people, you get more joy in return. You should give a good thought to the happiness that you can give out." –Eleanor Roosevelt

*****

"When you change your thoughts, remember to also change your world." –Norman Vincent Peale

*****

"It is only when we take chances that our lives improve. The initial and the most difficult risk we need to take is to become honest." –Walter Anderson

*****

"Nature has given us all the pieces required to achieve exceptional wellness and health but has left it to us to put these pieces together." –Diane McLaren

*****

"Success is not final; failure is not fatal: It is the courage to continue that counts." –Winston Churchill

*****

"It is better to fail in originality than to succeed in imitation." –Herman Melville

*****

"The road to success and the road to failure are almost exactly the same." –Colin R. Davis

*****

"Success usually comes to those who are too busy to be looking for it." –Henry David Thoreau

*****

"Develop success from failures. Discouragement and failure are two of the surest stepping stones to success." –Dale Carnegie

*****

"Nothing in the world can take the place of persistence. Talent will not; nothing is more common than unsuccessful men with talent. Genius will not; unrewarded genius is almost a proverb. Education will not; the world is full of educated derelicts. The slogan 'Press On' has solved and always will solve the problems of the human race." –Calvin Coolidge

*****

"There are three ways to ultimate success: The first way is to be kind. The second way is to be kind. The third way is to be kind." –Mister Rogers

*****

"Success is peace of mind, which is a direct result of self-satisfaction in knowing you made the effort to become the best of which you are capable." –John Wooden

*****

"I never dreamed about success. I worked for it." –Estée Lauder

*****

"Success is getting what you want; happiness is wanting what you get."—W. P. Kinsella

*****

Reference: https://www.shopify.com/blog/motivational-quotes

*****

"The pessimist sees difficulty in every opportunity. The optimist sees opportunity in every difficulty." –Winston Churchill

*****

"Don't let yesterday take up too much of today." –Will Rogers

*****

"You learn more from failure than from success. Don't let it stop you. Failure builds character." –Unknown

*****

"If you are working on something that you really care about, you don't have to be pushed. The vision pulls you." –Steve Jobs

*****

"Experience is a hard teacher because she gives the test first, the lesson afterward." —Vernon Sanders Law

*****

"To know how much there is to know is the beginning of learning to live." –Dorothy West

*****

"Goal setting is the secret to a compelling future." –Tony Robbins

*****

"Concentrate all your thoughts upon the work in hand. The sun's rays do not burn until brought to a focus." –Alexander Graham Bell

*****

"Either you run the day or the day runs you." –Jim Rohn

*****

"I'm a great believer in luck, and I find the harder I work, the more I have of it." –Thomas Jefferson

*****

"When we strive to become better than we are, everything around us becomes better too." –Paulo Coelho

*****

"Opportunity is missed by most people because it is dressed in overalls and looks like work." –Thomas Edison

*****

"Setting goals is the first step in turning the invisible into the visible." –Tony Robbins

*****

"Your work is going to fill a large part of your life, and the only way to be truly satisfied is to do what you believe is great work. And the only way to do great work is to love what you do. If you haven't found it yet, keep looking. Don't settle. As with all matters of the heart, you'll know when you find it." –Steve Jobs

*****

"Women challenge the status quo because we are never it." –Cindy Gallop

*****

"We don't just sit around and wait for other people. We just make, and we do." –Arlan Hamilton

*****

"Think like a queen. A queen is not afraid to fail. Failure is another stepping stone to greatness." –Oprah Winfrey

*****

"The strongest actions for a woman is to love herself, be herself and shine amongst those who never believed she could." –Unknown

*****

"Whenever you see a successful woman, look out for three men who are going out of their way to try to block her." – Yulia Tymoshenko

*****

"Some women choose to follow men, and some choose to follow their dreams. If you're wondering which way to go, remember that your career will never wake up and tell you that it doesn't love you anymore." –Lady Gaga

*****

"The thing women have yet to learn is nobody gives you power. You just take it." — Roseanne Barr

*****

"If they don't give you a seat at the table, bring a folding chair." —Shirley Chisholm

*****

"I raise up my voice–not so that I can shout, but so that those without a voice can be heard. ... We cannot all succeed when half of us are held back." — Malala Yousafzai

*****

"When a woman becomes her own best friend, life is easier." –Diane Von Furstenberg

*****

"If you want something said, ask a man; if you want something done, ask a woman." –Margaret Thatcher

*****

"We need women at all levels, including the top, to change the dynamic, reshape the conversation, to make sure women's voices are heard and heeded, not overlooked and ignored." –Sheryl Sandberg

*****

"It took me quite a long time to develop a voice, and now that I have it, I am not going to be silent." –Madeleine Albright

*****

"Women must learn to play the game as men do." –Eleanor Roosevelt

*****

"I swear, by my life and my love of it, that I will never live for the sake of another man, nor ask another man to live for mine." –Ayn Rand

*****

"He who conquers himself is the mightiest warrior." –Confucius

*****

"Try not to become a man of success, but rather become a man of value." –Albert Einstein

*****

"One man with courage makes a majority." –Andrew Jackson

*****

"One secret of success in life is for a man to be ready for his opportunity when it comes." –Benjamin Disraeli

*****

"A man who has committed a mistake and doesn't correct it is committing another mistake." –Confucius Kongzi

*****

"The successful man will profit from his mistakes and try again in a different way." –Dale Carnegie

*****

"A successful man is one who can lay a firm foundation with the bricks others have thrown at him." –David Brinkley

*****

"He is a wise man who does not grieve for the things which he has not, but rejoices for those which he has." –Epictetus

*****

"You've got to get up every morning with determination if you're going to go to bed with satisfaction." –George Lorimer

*****

"Education is the most powerful weapon which you can use to change the world." –Nelson Mandela

*****

"The most difficult thing is the decision to act; the rest is merely tenacity." –Amelia Earhart

*****

"You'll find that education is just about the only thing lying around loose in this world, and it's about the only thing a fellow can have as much of as he's willing to haul away." –John Graham

*****

"Take the attitude of a student, never be too big to ask questions, never know too much to learn something new." –Augustine Og Mandino

*****

"It is remarkable how much long-term advantage people like us have gotten by trying to be consistently not stupid, instead of trying to be very intelligent." –Charlie Munger

*****

"You can't be that kid standing at the top of the waterslide, overthinking it. You have to go down the chute." –Tina Fey

*****

"When I believe in something, I'm like a dog with a bone." –Melissa McCarthy

*****

"And the day came when the risk to remain tight in a bud was more painful than the risk it took to blossom." –Anaïs Nin

*****

"The standard you walk past is the standard you accept." –David Hurley

*****

"I've searched all the parks in all the cities and found no statues of committees." –Gilbert K. Chesterton

*****

"Success is stumbling from failure to failure with no loss of enthusiasm." —Winston Churchill

*****

"Keep your eyes on the stars, and your feet on the ground." —Theodore Roosevelt

*****

"Do not stop thinking of life as an adventure. You have no security unless you can live bravely, excitingly, imaginatively; unless you can choose a challenge instead of competence." —Eleanor Roosevelt

*****

"Perfection is not attainable. But if we chase perfection we can catch excellence." –Vince Lombardi

*****

"Get a good idea and stay with it. Dog it, and work at it until it's done right." –Walt Disney

*****

"Optimism is the faith that leads to achievement. Nothing can be done without hope and confidence." –Helen Keller

*****

"The elevator to success is out of order. You'll have to use the stairs, one step at a time." –Joe Girard

*****

"Be a positive energy trampoline–absorb what you need and rebound more back." –Dave Carolan

*****

"People often say that motivation doesn't last. Well, neither does bathing–that's why we recommend it daily." –Zig Ziglar

*****

“Work until your bank account looks like a phone number.” –Unknown

*****

“I am so clever that sometimes I don’t understand a single word of what I am saying.” –Oscar Wilde

*****

“People say nothing is impossible, but I do nothing every day.” –Winnie the Pooh

*****

“Life is like a sewer ... what you get out of it depends on what you put into it.” –Tom Lehrer

*****

“I always wanted to be somebody, but now I realize I should have been more specific.” –Lily Tomlin

*****

“Talent wins games, but teamwork and intelligence win championships.” –Michael Jordan

*****

“Individual commitment to a group effort–that is what makes a team work, a company work, a society work, a civilization work.” –Vince Lombardi

*****

“Teamwork is the ability to work together toward a common vision. The ability to direct individual accomplishments toward organizational objectives. It is the fuel that allows common people to attain uncommon results.” –Andrew Carnegie

*****

"Coming together is a beginning. Keeping together is progress. Working together is success." –Henry Ford

*****

"Alone we can do so little, together we can do so much." –Helen Keller

*****

"Remember, teamwork begins by building trust. And the only way to do that is to overcome our need for invulnerability." –Patrick Lencioni

*****

"I invite everyone to choose forgiveness rather than division, teamwork over personal ambition." –Jean-Francois Cope

*****

Short motivational quotes

*****

"Just one small positive thought in the morning can change your whole day." –Dalai Lama

*****

"Opportunities don't happen, you create them." –Chris Grosser

*****

"Love your family, work super hard, live your passion." –Gary Vaynerchuk

*****

"It is never too late to be what you might have been." –George Eliot

*****

"Don't let someone else's opinion of you become your reality." –Les Brown

*****

"If you're not positive energy, you're negative energy." –Mark Cuban

*****

"I am not a product of my circumstances. I am a product of my decisions." –Stephen R. Covey

*****

"Do the best you can. No one can do more than that." —John Wooden

*****

"If you can dream it, you can do it." —Walt Disney

*****

"Do what you can, with what you have, where you are." —Theodore Roosevelt

*****

"The greatest discovery of my generation is that a human being can alter his life by altering his attitudes." –William James

*****

"One of the differences between some successful and unsuccessful people is that one group is full of doers, while the other is full of wishers." –Edmond Mbiaka

*****

"I'd rather regret the things I've done than regret the things I haven't done." –Lucille Ball

*****

"You cannot plow a field by turning it over in your mind. To begin, begin." —Gordon B. Hinckley.

*****

"When you arise in the morning, think of what a privilege it is to be alive, to think, to enjoy, to love." –Marcus Aurelius

*****

"Mondays offer new beginnings 52 times a year!" –David Dweck

*****

"Be miserable. Or motivate yourself. Whatever has to be done, it's always your choice." –Wayne Dyer

*****

"Your Monday morning thoughts set the tone for your whole week. See yourself getting stronger, and living a fulfilling, happier, and healthier life." –Germany Kent

*****

"Friday sees more smiles than any other day of the workweek!" –Kate Summers

*****

"Oh! It's Friday again. Share the love that was missing during the week. In a worthy moment of peace and bliss." –S. O' Sade

*****

"Every Friday, I like to high-five myself for getting through another week on little more than caffeine, willpower, and inappropriate humor." –Nanea Hoffman

*****

"Make a Friday a day to celebrate work well done that you can be proud of, knowing that you just didn't put in time to the next paycheck." –Byron Pulsifer

*****

You will never be criticized by someone who is doing more than you. You will only be criticized by someone who is doing less than you. So, keep flying.

*****

A broken heart can heal but the scars always remain.

*****

If you find someone who is good, stop looking for someone better. Good people are hard to find.

*****

When doors close is not always punishment, it is re-direction to something greater.

*****

Learn to be done with people.

*****

Stop outsourcing your value.

*****

Trying to rewrite what is done only deepen the wound.

*****

Just because there is a race, doesn't mean you have to run it for not every path is yours to follow.

*****

Your growth terrifies people who are committed to staying the same. So, don't shrink for their comfort.

*****

The more you grow, the more their masks fall off.

*****

Growth isn't just elevation; it is about elimination.

*****

You will lose people on your way up, not because you have changed for worse but because your growth exposes their stagnation.

*****

Stop looking for who is not looking for you.

*****

Stop begging for attention, love, or support.

*****

Stop saying more than necessary. Silence is powerful.

*****

Listen first then speak.

*****

Not everyone thinks about you as much as you do.

*****

When you focus on problems you have more problems. When you focus on possibilities you have more opportunities.

*****

You meet people for a reason. Either you meet them to change your life or they meet you to change their life.

*****

If you do not have control of your mouth, you do not have control of your future.

*****

Do not have negative mind against your parents.

*****

Stop watering dead garden.

*****

You can heal your life.

*****

The most important person in your life is you.

*****

Every relationship good or bad taught you who you are and what you deserve.

*****

Let go of resentment but embrace those who hurt on purpose.

*****

Forgive those who caused you pain, their actions made you stronger and wiser.

*****

Sometimes the loudest answer is the one you don't give.

*****

Silence isn't weakness, it is power, it is growth let them talk.

*****

Stop arguing not because you have given up, but because you have grown up.

*****

Remember every reaction is a transaction.

*****

A good man is hard to find and hard to keep.

*****

When a good man leaves, he will not only find someone better, but he will be happier too.

*****

Don't ever, ever underestimate a good man in general.

*****

A man is as he is thinking.

*****

If someone wants you in their life, they will do everything to keep you in and if they don't want you in their life, absolutely nothing you do would change their mind.

*****

When two people care about each other they will always make it work.

*****

So many people are in love but not together.

*****

Don't waste your precious time on a wrong person.

*****

Eat your food as medicine, otherwise you will eat medicine as your food.

*****

Spot weak character early of suffer later. Weak characters destroy relationships.

*****

Walk away early not when you are broken.

*****

Stop looking for happiness in other people. You won't find it.

*****

You can use what you have to get what you don't have.

*****

Change happens when your mind is irrigated with new ideas.

*****

Success is the best reaction. Rise so high they cannot reach you.

*****

Time destroys the weak.

*****

Accept what you cannot control.

*****

Embrace the pain but don't let it define you.

*****

The past is gone, and future is uncertain.

*****

People talk about you because they lack the ability to talk with you.

*****

Your life doesn't not get better by chance. It gets better by change.

*****

The only person you are destined to become is the person you decide to be.

*****

If you don't know who you are, people will make you who you are not.

*****

Hardships often prepare ordinary people for an extraordinary destiny.

*****

Do one thing every day that scares you.

*****

Disruptive thinking will get you out of your comfort zone.

*****

Don't be pushed around by your fears in your mind.

*****

You are never too old to set another goal.

*****

Knowing your self is the beginning of all wisdom.

*****

Celebrate small successes, it will help you to fulfil your bigger dreams.

*****

The only thing we must fear is fear itself.

*****

The only impossible journey is the one you never begin.

*****

Challenges are what makes life interesting and overcoming them is what makes life meaningful.

*****

"Believe you can, and you're halfway there".

*****

Every time you fall remember to rise again.

*****

We must not be defeated by many defeats.

*****

Do what the clock does. Keep going.

*****

Getting started gets you ahead.

*****

Always dream big and dare to fail.

*****

If you do not stop, it doesn't matter how slowly you go.

*****

Always keep your face towards the sunshine and shadows will fall behind you.

*****

Quit talking and begin doing. It will get you started.

*****

Don't let your yesterday take up too much of your today.

*****

The future belongs to those who believe in their dreams.

*****

Opportunities don't happen; you create them.

*****

The best revenge is massive success, Keep flying.

*****

In the middle of every difficulty lies opportunity.

*****

A person who never made a mistake is the one who never tried anything.

*****

What we think we become.

*****

Love what you do, you will do great work.

*****

What you do makes difference. Stop doing nothing.

*****

Success is not the key to happiness. Happiness is the key to success.

*****

There is always a time to plant and time to harvest.

*****

If you want to lift yourself up, lift someone else.

*****

Happiness is not something readymade, it comes from your own action.

*****

You don't have to wait to be confident. Just do it and eventually confidence will follow.

*****

Without struggle there is no progress.

*****

Change brings opportunities.

*****

People who are crazy enough to think you can change the world are the one who do.

*****

Even the wisest mind withers away if it is always thinking about small things.

*****

Everyone you will ever meet knows something you don't. Knowing this will help you.

*****

Seek to turn mirrors into windows.

*****

Invest in knowledge it will pay you the best interest.

*****

Invest in personal development.

*****

Failure is not the opposite of success. It is a steppingstone towards it.

*****

We are products of our past, but we don't have to be prisoners of it.

*****

The best strategy to survive in the land of Eskimos is to bend down even if you know you are tall.

*****

Don't think about doing things. Just get them done. If people hate them make even more things. Don't worry about criticisms.

*****

To live is the rearrest thing in the world. Most people just exist.

*****

Do not allow other people's limited perceptions to define you.

*****

The forestry change but the monkeys remain the same doing the same thing again and again.

*****

You don't get taller by lowering the ruler.

*****

We live in a time when we call wrong right and right wrong.

*****

The greatest weapon you can use on your enemy is wisdom.

*****

Don't let people who do what you do surround you. They end up competing instead of building you.

*****

Do not live in a prison of people's perception.

*****

The longest journey starts with a single step.

*****

Chose your friends carefully. Most of them are only with you to fulfill their own agenda.

*****

We have a power to change our life.

*****

Your performance is always a problem to other people. They will try to bring you down.

*****

Ideas only grow when they are challenged.

*****

In building teamwork, remember the power of diversity.

*****

Don't avoid changes but embrace them.

*****

There is always a union between stability and fruitfulness.

*****

Failure is an opportunity to grow.

*****

Getting things done is more important than too much planning.

*****

Reading with a purpose open door to new thinking, new ideas and new wisdom.

*****

Always write things down so they become real.

*****

Always set goals. They give you direction on what to do.

*****

Always feed your mind with wonders. What you feed your mind becomes your reality.

*****

One of the most powerful ways to wire your brain for more joy and less stress is to focus on gratitude.

*****

Give yourself time to relax, to make your mind creative.

*****

Giving will change your life.

*****

Listening makes you learn more and solve problems more effectively.

*****

Believe in process. Great things always take time to happen.

*****

You are the average of five people you spend time with.

*****

Your environment will either lift you up or bring you down.

*****

"When you leave work on Friday, leave work. Don't let technology follow you throughout your weekend (answering text messages and emails). Take a break. You will be more refreshed to begin the workweek if you have had a break." –Catherine Pulsifer

*****

"You can get everything in life you want if you will just help enough other people get what they want." –Zig Ziglar

*****

"Inspiration does exist, but it must find you working." –Pablo Picasso

*****

"Don't settle for average. Bring your best to the moment. Then, whether it fails or succeeds, at least you know you gave all you had." –Angela Bassett

*****

"Show up, show up, show up, and after a while the muse shows up, too." –Isabel Allende

*****

"Don't bunt. Aim out of the ballpark. Aim for the company of immortals." —David Ogilvy

*****

"I have stood on a mountain of no's for one yes." –Barbara Elaine Smith

*****

"If you believe something needs to exist, if it's something you want to use yourself, don't let anyone ever stop you from doing it." –Tobias Lütke

*****

"Don't look at your feet to see if you are doing it right. Just dance." —Anne Lamott

*****

"Someone's sitting in the shade today because someone planted a tree a long time ago." –Warren Buffet

*****

"True freedom is impossible without a mind made free by discipline." —Mortimer J. Adler

*****

"Rivers know this: there is no hurry. We shall get there someday." —A. A. Milne

*****

"There is a vitality, a life force, an energy, a quickening that is translated through you into action, and because there is only one of you in all time, this expression is unique. And if you block it, it will never exist through any other medium and will be lost." —Martha Graham

*****

"Small is not just a stepping stone. Small is a great destination itself." —Jason Fried

*****

"He that can have patience can have what he will." —Benjamin Franklin

*****

"The only one who can tell you 'you can't win' is you, and you don't have to listen." –Jessica Ennis

*****

"Set your goals high, and don't stop till you get there." –Bo Jackson

*****

"Take your victories, whatever they may be, cherish them, use them, but don't settle for them." –Mia Hamm

*****

"Life can be much broader once you discover one simple fact: Everything around you that you call life was made up by people that were no smarter than you. And you can change it, you can influence it. ... Once you learn that, you'll never be the same again." –Steve Jobs

*****

"Life is like riding a bicycle. To keep your balance, you must keep moving." –Albert Einstein

*****

"What you do speaks so loudly that I cannot hear what you say." –Ralph Waldo Emerson

*****

"I have never let my schooling interfere with my education." –Mark Twain

*****

"If you can't yet do great things, do small things in a great way." —Napoleon Hill

*****

"If you really want to do something, you'll find a way. If you don't, you'll find an excuse." —Jim Rohn

*****

"Be sure you put your feet in the right place, then stand firm." —Abraham Lincoln

*****

"Live out of your imagination, not your history." –Stephen Covey

*****

"Do not wait for the perfect time and place to enter, for you are already onstage." –Unknown

*****

"The greater the difficulty, the more the glory in surmounting it." —Epicurus

*****

"Courage doesn't always roar. Sometimes courage is a quiet voice at the end of the day saying, 'I will try again tomorrow.'" –Mary Anne Radmacher

*****

"If the decisions you make about where you invest your blood, sweat, and tears are not consistent with the person you aspire to be, you'll never become that person." —Clayton M. Christensen

*****

"Fear of what other people will think is the single most paralyzing dynamic in business and in life. The best moment of my life was the day I realized that I no longer give a damn what anybody thinks. That's enormously liberating and freeing, and it's the only way to live your life and do your business" –Cindy Gallop

*****

"The only way of discovering the limits of the possible is to venture a little way past them into the impossible." —Arthur C. Clarke

*****

"Worry is a misuse of imagination." –Unknown

*****

"Courage is the most important of all the virtues because, without courage, you can't practice any other virtue consistently." —Maya Angelou

*****

"I never look back, darling. It distracts from the now." – Edna Mode

*****

"A year from now you will wish you had started today." – Unknown

*****

"The reason we struggle with insecurity is because we compare our behind the scenes with everyone else's highlight reel." –Steve Furtick

*****

"Somewhere, something incredible is waiting to be known." –Carl Sagan

*****

"I will not lose, for even in defeat, there's a valuable lesson learned, so it evens up for me." –Jay-Z

*****

"I do not try to dance better than anyone else. I only try to dance better than myself." –Arianna Huffington

*****

"If you don't risk anything, you risk even more." –Erica Jong

*****

"Failure is simply the opportunity to begin again, this time more intelligently." –Henry Ford

*****

"Our greatest glory is not in never falling, but in rising every time we fall." –Confucius

*****

"If you change the way you look at things, the things you look at change." –Wayne Dyer

*****

"We must reach out our hand in friendship and dignity, both to those who would befriend us and those who would be our enemy." –Arthur Ashe

*****

"It's fine to celebrate success, but it is more important to heed the lessons of failure." –

*****

Bill Gates

*****

"I can't tell you how many times I've been given a no, only to find that a better, brighter, bigger yes was right around the corner." –Arlan Hamilton

*****

"We need to accept that we won't always make the right decisions, that we'll screw up royally sometimes– understanding that failure is not the opposite of success, it's part of success." –Ariana Huffington

*****

"When everything seems to be going against you, remember that the airplane takes off against the wind, not with it." –Henry Ford

*****

"You cannot always control what goes on outside. But you can always control what goes on inside." –Wayne Dyer

*****

"We are what we repeatedly do. Excellence, then, is not an act, but a habit." –Aristotle

*****

"Start where you are. Use what you have. Do what you can." –Arthur Ashe

*****

"Hustle beats talent when talent doesn't hustle." –Ross Simmonds

*****

"Everything you've ever wanted is sitting on the other side of fear." –George Addair

*****

"The question isn't who is going to let me; it's who is going to stop me." –Ayn Rand

*****

"Every strike brings me closer to the next home run." –Babe Ruth

*****

"I have not failed. I've just found 10,000 ways that won't work." –Thomas Edison

*****

"Don't worry about failure; you only have to be right once." –Drew Houston

*****

"You carry the passport to your own happiness." –Diane Von Furstenberg

*****

"Never let success get to your head, and never let failure get to your heart." –Drake

*****

"Ideation without execution is delusion." –Robin Sharma

*****

"Make sure your worst enemy doesn't live between your own two ears." –Laird Hamilton

*****

"It is a rough road that leads to the heights of greatness." –Lucius Annaeus Seneca

*****

"For the great doesn't happen through impulse alone, and is a succession of little things that are brought together." –Vincent Van Gogh

*****

"If we take care of the moments, the years will take care of themselves." –Maria Edgeworth

*****

"Resilience is when you address uncertainty with flexibility." –Unknown

*****

"Sometimes magic is just someone spending more time on something than anyone else might reasonably expect." –Raymond Joseph Teller

*****

"It's not the will to win that matters–everyone has that. It's the will to prepare to win that matters." –Paul Bryant

*****

"As a single footstep will not make a path on the earth, so a single thought will not make a pathway in the mind. To make a deep physical path, we walk again and again. To make a deep mental path, we must think over and over the kind of thoughts we wish to dominate our lives." –Henry David Thoreau

*****

"Never give up on a dream just because of the time it will take to accomplish it. The time will pass anyway." –Earl Nightingale

*****

"True humility is not thinking less of yourself; it is thinking of yourself less." –Unknown

*****

"The two most important days in your life are the day you're born and the day you find out why." –Mark Twain.

*****

"Nothing ever goes away until it teaches us what we need to know." –Pema Chodron

*****

"We can see through others only when we can see through ourselves." –Bruce Lee

*****

"First, forget inspiration. Habit is more dependable. Habit will sustain you whether you're inspired or not. Habit will help you finish and polish your stories. Inspiration won't. Habit is persistence in practice." —Octavia Butler

*****

"The best way out is always through." —Robert Frost

*****

"The battles that count aren't the ones for gold medals. The struggles within yourself–the invisible, inevitable battles inside all of us–that's where it's at." –Jesse Owens

*****

"If there is no struggle, there is no progress." –Frederick Douglass

*****

"Someone will declare, 'I am the leader!' and expect everyone to get in line and follow him or her to the gates of heaven or hell. My experience is that it doesn't happen that way. Others follow you based on the quality of your actions rather than the magnitude of your declarations." —Bill Walsh

*****

"Courage is like a muscle. We strengthen it by use." – Ruth Gordo

*****

"Relentlessly prune bullshit, don't wait to do things that matter, and savor the time you have. That's what you do when life is short." –Paul Graham

*****

"More is lost by indecision than wrong decision." – Marcus Tullius Cicero

*****

"If the highest aim of a captain were to preserve his ship, he would keep it in port forever." –Thomas Aquinas

*****

"You can be the ripest, juiciest peach in the world, and there's still going to be somebody who hates peaches." –Dita Von Teese

*****

"Keep a little fire burning; however small, however hidden." —Cormac McCarthy

*****

"You'll never get bored when you try something new. There's really no limit to what you can do." –Dr. Seuss

*****

"I think it's intoxicating when somebody is so unapologetically who they are." –Don Cheadle

*****

"You can never leave footprints that last if you are always walking on tiptoe." –Leymah Gbowee

*****

"If you don't like the road you're walking, start paving another one." –Dolly Parton

*****

"If it makes you nervous, you're doing it right." –Childish Gambino

*****

"What you do makes a difference, and you have to decide what kind of difference you want to make." –Jane Goodall

*****

"I choose to make the rest of my life the best of my life." –Louise Hay

*****

"In order to be irreplaceable one must always be different." –Coco Chanel

*****

"Anything can make me stop and look and wonder, and sometimes learn." –Kurt Vonnegut

*****

"People's passion and desire for authenticity is strong." –Constance Wu

*****

"A surplus of effort could overcome a deficit of confidence." –Sonia Sotomayor

*****

"Doubt is a killer. You just have to know who you are and what you stand for." –Jennifer Lopez

*****

"No one changes the world who isn't obsessed." –Billie Jean King

*****

"I learned a long time ago that there is something worse than missing the goal, and that's not pulling the trigger." –Mia Hamm

*****

"Some people want it to happen, some wish it would happen, others make it happen." –Michael Jordan

*****

"Every accomplishment starts with the decision to try." - John F. Kennedy

*****

"Growth is painful. Change is painful. But nothing is as painful as staying stuck somewhere you don't belong." - Mandy Hale

*****

"Climb mountains not so the world can see you, but so you can see the world." - David McCullough Jr.

*****

"Keep going. Everything you need will come to you at the perfect time." - Unknown

*****

"Do not despise small beginnings." - Zechariah 4:10

*****

"The man on top of the mountain didn't fall there." - Vince Lombardi

*****

"You won't always be motivated, so you must learn to be disciplined." - Unknown

*****

"You didn't come this far to only come this far." - Unknown

*****

"Success doesn't rush. The greatest reward is the journey." - Jeff Moore

*****

"Keep your face always toward the sunshine—and shadows will fall behind you." - Walt Whitman

*****

"A little progress each day adds up to big results." - Satya Nani

*****

"When you feel like quitting, think about why you started." - Unknown

*****

"Doubt kills more dreams than failure ever will." - Suzy Kassem

*****

"If you're not willing to risk the usual, you'll have to settle for the ordinary." - Jim Rohn

*****

"Success is not final, failure is not fatal: It is the courage to continue that counts." - Winston Churchill

*****

"Don't watch the clock; do what it does. Keep going." - Sam Levenson

*****

"The only place where success comes before work is in the dictionary." - Vidal Sassoon

*****

"It always seems impossible until it's done." - Nelson Mandela

*****

"Hardships often prepare ordinary people for an extraordinary destiny." - C.S. Lewis

*****

"The way to get started is to quit talking and begin doing." - Walt Disney

*****

"Dream big and dare to fail." - Norman Vaughan

*****

"Success usually comes to those who are too busy to be looking for it." - Henry David Thoreau

*****

"Don't be afraid to give up the good to go for the great." - John D. Rockefeller

*****

"I find that the harder I work, the more luck I seem to have." - Thomas Jefferson

*****

"Success is walking from failure to failure with no loss of enthusiasm." - Winston Churchill

*****

"Act as if what you do makes a difference. It does." – William James

*****

"Your time is limited, so don't waste it living someone else's life." – Steve Jobs

*****

"You miss 100% of the shots you don't take." – Wayne Gretzky

*****

"Success isn't just about what you accomplish, it's about what you inspire others to do." – Unknown

*****

"Believe you can and you're halfway there." – Theodore Roosevelt

*****

"Everything you've ever wanted is on the other side of fear." – George Addair

*****

"The future belongs to those who believe in the beauty of their dreams." – Eleanor Roosevelt

*****

"Don't limit your challenges. Challenge your limits." – Jerry Dunn

*****

"Push yourself, because no one else is going to do it for you." – Unknown

*****

"The best revenge is massive success." - Frank Sinatra

*****

"Success is not in what you have, but who you are." - Bo Bennett

*****

"Opportunities don't happen. You create them." - Chris Grosser

*****

"You are never too old to set another goal or to dream a new dream." - C.S. Lewis

*****

"Do one thing every day that scares you." - Eleanor Roosevelt

*****

"Only those who dare to fail greatly can ever achieve greatly." - Robert F. Kennedy

*****

"I never dreamed about success. I worked for it." - Estée Lauder

*****

"Success is the sum of small efforts, repeated day in and day out." - Robert Collier

*****

"Try not to become a man of success. Rather become a man of value." - Albert Einstein

*****

"The only limit to our realization of tomorrow is our doubts of today." – Franklin D. Roosevelt

*****

"If you want to achieve greatness stop asking for permission." – Unknown

*****

"What you get by achieving your goals is not as important as what you become by achieving your goals." – Zig Ziglar

*****

"I attribute my success to this: I never gave or took any excuse." – Florence Nightingale

*****

"In the middle of every difficulty lies opportunity." – Albert Einstein

*****

"Do not be embarrassed by your failures, learn from them and start again." – Richard Branson

*****

"A goal without a plan is just a wish." – Antoine de Saint-Exupéry

*****

"Start where you are. Use what you have. Do what you can." – Arthur Ashe

*****

"Success is how high you bounce when you hit bottom." – George S. Patton

*****

"Don't wait. The time will never be just right." – Napoleon Hill

*****

"Success is liking yourself, liking what you do, and liking how you do it." – Maya Angelou

*****

"There is no elevator to success – you have to take the stairs." – Zig Ziglar

*****

"If you're going through hell, keep going." – Winston Churchill

*****

"Don't be pushed by your problems, be led by your dreams." – Ralph Waldo Emerson

*****

"Success does not consist in never making mistakes but in never making the same one a second time." – George Bernard Shaw

*****

"Be patient with yourself. You are growing stronger every day." – Unknown

*****

"The climb might be tough, but the view from the top is worth it." – Unknown

*****

"Your struggle today is your strength tomorrow." – Tim Fargo

*****

"Focus on how far you've come, not how far you have to go." - Unknown

*****

"Success doesn't come from what you do occasionally, it comes from what you do consistently." - Marie Forleo

*****

"Rise above the storm and you will find the sunshine." - Mario Fernández

*****

"Go as far as you can see; when you get there, you'll be able to see further." - Thomas Carlyle

*****

"The comeback is always stronger than the setback." - Unknown

*****

"Every step forward, no matter how small, is progress." - Unknown

*****

"Believe in your infinite potential. Your only limitations are those you set upon yourself." - Roy T. Bennett

*****

"Success is not about speed, it's about direction." - Unknown

*****

"Keep grinding. Stay persistent. Trust the process." - Eric Thomas

*****

"Don't compare your Chapter 1 to someone else's Chapter 20." - Jon Acuff

*****

"The best view comes after the hardest climb." - Unknown

*****

"You're not behind in life. There's no schedule or timeline you're supposed to follow." - Unknown

*****

"Fall in love with the process and the results will come." - Eric Thomas

*****

"Be proud of how far you've come, and have faith in how far you can go." - Christian Larson

*****

"Your life does not get better by chance, it gets better by change." - Jim Rohn

*****

"Your only competition is who you were yesterday." - Unknown

*****

"The pain you feel today will be the strength you feel tomorrow." - Unknown

*****

"Be patient. The best things happen unexpectedly." - Unknown

*****

"Focus on the step in front of you, not the whole staircase." - Unknown

*****

"You have to fight through some bad days to earn the best days of your life." - Unknown

*****

"Nothing changes if nothing changes." - Unknown

*****

"Keep your dreams alive. Understand that to achieve anything requires faith and belief in yourself." - Gail Devers

*****

"Effort is the bridge between goals and accomplishment." - Jim Rohn

*****

"Success takes time. Keep going even when no one is clapping." - Unknown

*****

"Discipline is choosing between what you want now and what you want most." - Abraham Lincoln

*****

"When it's tough, do it tough." - Les Brown

*****

"There is no growth in your comfort zone." - Unknown

*****

"Trust the process. The results will speak." - Unknown

*****

"Today's pain is tomorrow's power." - Robin Sharma

*****

"One day or day one. You decide." - Unknown

*****

"It doesn't matter how slowly you go as long as you don't stop." - Confucius

*****

"You are allowed to be both a masterpiece and a work in progress." - Sophia Bush

*****

"Just because you're struggling doesn't mean you're failing." - Unknown

*****

"The secret to getting ahead is getting started." - Mark Twain

*****

"Keep showing up. That's half the battle." - Unknown

*****

"Never give up on something you can't go a day without thinking about." - Winston Churchill

*****

"Even if you're on the right track, you'll get run over if you just sit there." - Will Rogers

*****

"Storms make trees take deeper roots." - Dolly Parton

*****

"Be stubborn about your goals and flexible about your methods." - Unknown

*****

"It's not who you are that holds you back. It's who you think you're not." - Denis Waitley

*****

"Run your own race. Stay in your lane." - Unknown

*****

"The elevator to success is out of order. You'll have to take the stairs." - Joe Girard

*****

"The real glow-up is becoming the person you're proud of." - Unknown

*****

"You don't have to see the whole picture–just take the next step." - Unknown

*****

"Small deeds done are better than great deeds planned." - Peter Marshall

*****

"Let your hustle be louder than your excuses." - Unknown

*****

"Your journey is unique. Don't let anyone else's path distract you from your own." - Unknown

*****

"You're doing better than you think." - Unknown

*****

"Life is tough, but so are you." - Unknown

*****

"Aim for progress, not perfection." - Unknown

*****

"You don't find willpower, you create it." - Unknown

*****

"A journey of a thousand miles begins with a single step." - Lao Tzu

*****

"What seems hard now will one day be your warm-up." - Unknown

*****

"If you get tired, learn to rest, not quit." - Banksy

*****

"Celebrate every win, no matter how small." - Unknown

*****

"Progress is still progress, no matter how slow." - Unknown

*****

"The moment you're ready to quit is usually the moment right before the miracle happens." - Unknown

*****

"Dreams don't work unless you do." - John C. Maxwell

*****

"Growth begins at the end of your comfort zone." - Tony Robbins

*****

"Make your future self proud." - Unknown

*****

"You are building something that didn't exist before–keep going." - Unknown

*****

"Don't be discouraged by how far you still have to go. Be proud of how far you've come." - Unknown

*****

"You were born to do more than just pay bills and die." - Unknown

*****

"No one is you, and that is your power." - Dave Grohl

*****

"Be the kind of person who makes others want to up their game." - Unknown

*****

"Your breakthrough is on the other side of not giving up." - Unknown

*****

"The key to success is to start before you're ready." - Marie Forleo

*****

"Sometimes courage is the quiet voice at the end of the day saying, 'I will try again tomorrow.'" - Mary Anne Radmacher

*****

"You are stronger than you think." - Unknown

*****

"It's okay to be a work in progress." - Unknown

*****

"What lies behind us and what lies before us are tiny matters compared to what lies within us." - Ralph Waldo Emerson

*****

"Everything is hard before it's easy." - Goethe

*****

"Each day is a new opportunity to improve." - Unknown

*****

"Stay patient and trust your journey." - Unknown

*****

"Make peace with where you are while keeping focus on where you're going." - Unknown

*****

"Sometimes the bravest thing you can do is just keep going." - Unknown

*****

"Become addicted to the feeling of bettering yourself." - Unknown

*****

"Stay hungry. Stay foolish." - Steve Jobs

*****

"One step at a time is all it takes to get you there." - Emily Dickinson

*****

"Let each success humble you and each failure teach you." - Unknown

*****

"Progress, not perfection." - Unknown

*****

"You can do hard things." - Glennon Doyle

*****

"Keep climbing. Your future self is already cheering you on." - Unknown

*****

You were born to be real, not to be perfect.

*****

Push yourself, because no one else is going to do it for you.

*****

Success doesn't come from what you do occasionally. It comes from what you do consistently.

*****

Don't limit your challenges. Challenge your limits.

*****

You don't have to be great to start, but you have to start to be great.

*****

Stay away from those people who try to disparage your ambitions.

*****

The harder you work for something, the greater you'll feel when you achieve it.

*****

Success is the sum of small efforts, repeated day in and day out.

*****

Dreams don't work unless you do.

*****

Great things never come from comfort zones.

*****

The key to success is to focus on goals, not obstacles.

*****

Strive for progress, not perfection.

*****

Don't wait for opportunity. Create it.

*****

Doubt kills more dreams than failure ever will.

*****

If it doesn't challenge you, it won't change you.

*****

Hustle until your haters ask if you're hiring.

*****

You are capable of more than you know.

*****

Little by little, a little becomes a lot.

*****

Your only limit is your mind.

*****

Turn your wounds into wisdom.

*****

Be stronger than your excuses.

*****

Learn as if you will live forever, live like you will die tomorrow.

*****

Don't count the days, make the days count.

*****

One day or day one. You decide.

*****

Discipline is doing what needs to be done even when you don't feel like doing it.

*****

You're only confined by the walls you build yourself.

*****

Don't be afraid to give up the good to go for the great.

*****

If you get tired, learn to rest, not quit.

*****

The best view comes after the hardest climb.

*****

Action is the foundational key to all success.

*****

Strength doesn’t come from what you can do. It comes from overcoming the things you thought you couldn’t.

*****

You don’t need to see the whole staircase, just take the first step.

*****

Don't fear failure. Fear being in the same place next year as you are today.

*****

If people are doubting how far you can go, go so far that you can’t hear them anymore.

*****

Do it with passion or not at all.

*****

Work hard in silence, let your success be your noise.

*****

Don’t be busy. Be productive.

*****

Opportunities don't happen. You create them.

*****

You are never too old to set another goal or to dream a new dream.

*****

Stop wishing. Start doing.

*****

The distance between dreams and reality is called action.

*****

Success is what comes after you stop making excuses.

*****

A river cuts through rock not because of its power but because of its persistence.

*****

Comfort is the enemy of achievement.

*****

The pain you feel today will be the strength you feel tomorrow.

*****

Don't watch the clock; do what it does—keep going.

*****

Be so good they can't ignore you.

*****

Courage doesn't always roar. Sometimes courage is the quiet voice at the end of the day saying, "I will try again tomorrow."

*****

The secret of getting ahead is getting started.

*****

Success is walking from failure to failure with no loss of enthusiasm.

*****

Your time is limited, so don't waste it living someone else's life.

*****

Don't let yesterday take up too much of today.

*****

Life is 10% what happens to us and 90% how we react to it.

*****

Winning isn't everything, but wanting to win is.

*****

The best way to predict the future is to create it.

*****

Fall seven times, stand up eight.

*****

Go the extra mile. It's never crowded.

*****

It always seems impossible until it's done.

*****

Never let the fear of striking out keep you from playing the game.

*****

Success is not in what you have, but who you are.

*****

Keep your eyes on the stars and your feet on the ground.

*****

Your life does not get better by chance, it gets better by change.

*****

Start where you are. Use what you have. Do what you can.

*****

The secret of your future is hidden in your daily routine.

*****

You have to fight through some bad days to earn the best days of your life.

*****

If you believe it will work out, you'll see opportunities.

*****

Keep grinding, stay consistent, and trust the process.

*****

Big journeys begin with small steps.

*****

Nobody cares. Work harder.

*****

Prove yourself to yourself, not others.

*****

A little progress each day adds up to big results.

*****

Make it happen. Shock everyone.

*****

Don't stop when you're tired. Stop when you're done.

*****

The comeback is always stronger than the setback.

*****

Everything you've ever wanted is on the other side of fear.

*****

Success doesn't find you. You have to go out and get it.

*****

You don't find the willpower you need. You create it.

*****

If you're going through hell, keep going.

*****

You must expect great things of yourself before you can do them.

*****

Be fearless in the pursuit of what sets your soul on fire.

*****

Be humble. Be hungry. And always be the hardest worker in the room.

*****

Focus on being productive instead of busy.

*****

A goal without a plan is just a wish.

*****

Chase your dreams but always know the road that'll lead you home again.

*****

The difference between ordinary and extraordinary is that little extra.

*****

Keep moving forward.

*****

Mindset is what separates the best from the rest.

*****

The harder the battle, the sweeter the victory.

*****

The dream is free. The hustle is sold separately.

*****

You've got what it takes, but it will take everything you've got.

*****

You are the author of your own success story.

*****

Strength grows in the moments when you think you can't go on but you keep going anyway.

*****

Today's accomplishments were yesterday's impossibilities.

*****

Fight for your dreams. Your future self will thank you.

*****

Just one small positive thought in the morning can change your whole day.

*****

Life rewards the risk-takers.

*****

Dare to be different. Dare to be you.

*****

Some people want it to happen, some wish it would happen, others make it happen.

*****

Even if you're on the right track, you'll get run over if you just sit there.

*****

Make yourself proud.

*****

A leader is one who knows the way, goes the way, and shows the way.

*****

Leadership is not about being in charge. It's about taking care of those in your charge.

*****

Vision is the art of seeing what is invisible to others.

*****

Leadership is not about being the best. It's about making everyone else better.

*****

A true leader has the confidence to stand alone, the courage to make tough decisions, and the compassion to listen to the needs of others.

*****

Strategic vision is not just about seeing ahead; it's about knowing how to navigate the path to success.

*****

Leadership is the capacity to translate vision into reality.

*****

The function of leadership is to produce more leaders, not more followers.

*****

Innovation distinguishes between a leader and a follower.

*****

A leader is a dealer in hope.

*****

The ability to learn is the most important quality a leader can have.

*****

Leadership is the ability to get extraordinary achievement from ordinary people.

*****

Leadership is not about being in control, it's about creating an environment where others can succeed.

*****

Leadership is not about being perfect, it's about being authentic and leading with integrity.

*****

Leadership is about influence, not authority.

*****

The key to successful leadership today is influence, not authority.

*****

Leaders don't create followers, they create more leaders.

*****

Great leaders are willing to sacrifice their own personal interests for the good of the team.

*****

Vision without action is merely a dream. Action without vision just passes the time. Vision with action can change the world.

*****

A great leader's courage to fulfill his vision comes from passion, not position.

*****

Leadership is not about being the loudest in the room, but being the one who listens the most.

*****

Leadership is not about being the best, but about making everyone else better.

*****

Strategic leadership is the ability to influence others to achieve a goal through visionary thinking and effective action.

*****

The price of greatness is responsibility.

*****

It's not about having a vision; it's about having the courage to follow it.

*****

Leadership is about setting a vision and aligning the team to bring it to life.

*****

A visionary leader doesn't just look at the next few steps, but creates a path for generations to follow.

*****

A leader is one who can inspire others to dream more, learn more, do more, and become more.

*****

The only limit to our realization of tomorrow will be our doubts of today.

*****

Leadership means finding a way to get people to believe in the impossible.

*****

A visionary leader sees opportunities where others see obstacles.

*****

The challenge of leadership is to be strong, but not rude; be kind, but not weak; be bold, but not a bully; be thoughtful, but not lazy; be humble, but not timid; be proud, but not arrogant; have humor, but without folly.

*****

Leadership is unlocking people's potential to become better.

*****

The art of leadership is saying no, not yes. It is very easy to say yes.

*****

Leaders are not born; they are made.

*****

A great leader doesn't lead by power or control but by influence and trust.

*****

The best leaders are those who are willing to serve.

*****

A strategic leader sees the future and guides others toward it with confidence.

*****

A leader's job is not to be in charge, but to take care of those in their charge.

*****

To lead people, walk behind them.

*****

The greatest leaders don't just lead; they make the people around them feel like they are leaders, too.

*****

Leadership is not a position or a title, it's action and example.

*****

The sign of a great leader is the ability to turn a problem into an opportunity.

*****

The best way to find out if you can trust somebody is to trust them.

*****

Vision without execution is just hallucination.

*****

A leader leads by example, not by force.

*****

Strategic leadership is not only about setting direction but about inspiring others to follow it.

*****

Leadership is about seeing possibilities where others only see limitations.

*****

The true test of leadership is how well you function in a crisis.

*****

Leadership is the ability to make difficult decisions when others hesitate.

*****

The best leaders are those who remain calm in the face of adversity.

*****

Leadership is not about being the smartest in the room but about empowering others to do their best work.

*****

True leaders don't create followers; they create more leaders.

*****

A good leader leads the people from above them. A great leader leads the people from within them.

*****

A leader is one who can see the future and inspire others to get there.

*****

A true leader's job is to inspire and empower others to do what they thought was impossible.

*****

Visionary leadership is about creating a future that others can rally behind.

*****

The greatest leaders are those who create the conditions for others to succeed.

*****

Leaders must be able to translate vision into action.

*****

Leadership is about listening, learning, and adapting.

*****

The most important thing in leadership is not about being right; it's about doing what's right.

*****

A visionary leader understands the power of people and aims to unlock their potential.

*****

Leadership is not about being the most powerful person; it's about empowering others.

*****

The function of leadership is to create more leaders, not more followers.

*****

A true leader is one who leads by example and inspires others to follow.

*****

Strategic leaders look beyond the immediate horizon to plan for future opportunities.

*****

You cannot lead others if you do not lead yourself first.

*****

Leadership requires a vision and a willingness to act on that vision.

*****

A leader is someone who can motivate others to do things they never thought possible.

*****

Leaders must see the big picture while focusing on the small details.

*****

Leadership is about creating an environment that nurtures growth, innovation, and development.

*****

True leaders empower others to step up and lead.

*****

A great leader is someone who can inspire confidence in others.

*****

Leadership is about creating a sense of purpose and helping others find their way.

*****

Visionary leadership is about setting a bold direction and taking risks to get there.

*****

Leadership is about getting people to do things that they didn't think they could do.

*****

A great leader is one who listens, understands, and acts on what they hear.

*****

True leadership is about making a difference in the lives of others.

*****

The best leaders are those who lift others up and inspire them to achieve more.

*****

Leadership is about taking responsibility, not making excuses.

*****

A visionary leader knows where they want to go, and can inspire others to join them.

*****

Leadership is about leading by example and showing others the way forward.

*****

A good leader takes the time to understand the strengths and weaknesses of those they lead.

*****

Visionary leaders turn their dreams into plans, and their plans into reality.

*****

Leadership is not about control, but about creating opportunities for others.

*****

A true leader empowers people to lead themselves.

*****

A visionary leader's role is to create a culture of innovation and forward thinking.

*****

The ability to inspire others to act is the true measure of leadership.

*****

Leadership is about creating a shared vision and getting everyone on board to achieve it.

*****

Strategic leadership is about being able to navigate ambiguity and find clarity.

*****

The true measure of leadership is not how well you lead but how well you inspire others to lead.

*****

A great leader encourages others to see themselves as leaders.

*****

Leadership is not about titles, it's about influence.

*****

Leadership is about building relationships and creating an environment where people feel safe to take risks.

*****

Great leaders know when to lead and when to follow.

*****

A visionary leader brings the future into focus and takes others on the journey.

*****

True leadership is about having the courage to make difficult decisions for the greater good.

*****

Success is not the key to happiness. Happiness is the key to success. If you love what you are doing, you will be successful.

*****

Success usually comes to those who are too busy to be looking for it.

*****

The only place where success comes before work is in the dictionary.

*****

The way to get started is to quit talking and begin doing.

*****

I find that the harder I work, the more luck I seem to have.

*****

It is hard to fail, but it is worse never to have tried to succeed.

*****

The road to success and the road to failure are almost exactly the same.

*****

Success is not final, failure is not fatal: It is the courage to continue that counts.

*****

Success is to be measured not so much by the position that one has reached in life as by the obstacles which he has overcome.

*****

The secret of success is constancy to purpose.

*****

A person who never made a mistake never tried anything new.

*****

I never dreamed about success. I worked for it.

*****

Don't watch the clock; do what it does. Keep going.

*****

The only limit to our realization of tomorrow is our doubts of today.

*****

Eagles don't flap they soar. Your strength lies in silence, not noise.Emma-Empire

*****

Success is how high you bounce when you hit bottom.

*****

The best revenge is massive success.

*****

Success is liking yourself, liking what you do, and liking how you do it.

*****

Success is not the absence of failure; it's the persistence through failure.

*****

Every thing built on people shall come down.

*****

Keep your face always toward the sunshine–and shadows will fall behind you.

*****

The only limit to your impact is your imagination and commitment.

*****

To be successful, you must accept all challenges that come your way. You can't just accept the ones you like.

*****

Success is a journey, not a destination.

*****

To changer the world we must be good to those who cannot repay us.

*****

God's mission needs authentic people not just workers.

*****

Our service is God's calling.

*****

Things have a price and can be for sale, but people have dignity that is priceless and worth far more than things.

*****

We cannot sleep peacefully while babies are dying of hunger and the elderly are without medical assistance.

*****

Are you angry at someone? If so pray for that person.

*****

All lives have equal value.

*****

Every Soul is beautiful and precious, is worthy of dignity and respect and deserving of peace, joy and love.

*****

If our hearts are made of stones, the stones find their way into our hands, and we are ready to throw them.

*****

Money has to serve, not to rule.

*****

If money and material things become the center of our lives, they seizes us and make us slaves.

*****

It is God who gives life. Let us respect and love human life.

*****

Only love fills the empty spaces caused by evil.

*****

If we see someone who needs help, do we stop? There is so much suffering and poverty, and a great need for a good Samaritans.

*****

Success is not about what you have, but what you give.

*****

No one can grow if he doesn't accept his smallness.

*****

Cure sometimes, treat often, comfort always.

*****

Walking is man's best medicine.

*****

Natural forces within us are the true healers of disease.

*****

Be rich in love not money.

*****

Get your head high even when your heart is down.

*****

Real love doesn't need tittles.

*****

Do not allow bitterness to build in you when someone you love becomes everyone's love.

*****

The mind is the software of the body, and the external environment is the hardware.

*****

Humility is not weakness; it is the greatest strength.

*****

Don't be isolated by wealth, tittles, or money.

*****

Always build connections and not barriers.

*****

Our job is to build something that speaks louder than words.

*****

Putting people first can change everything.

*****

Leadership is not about power; it is a service.

*****

Avoid man with clean suit but dirty heart.

*****

As shepherds must smell the smell of his sheep, always be where the people you save.

*****

It is in the soil and dusts of the forgotten, among the poor where people teach you who God is.

*****

Do not chase the spotlight but keep the flame of love burning in the dark.

*****

A successful person is one who can lay a firm foundation with the bricks others have thrown at him or her.

*****

Success is not measured by what you accomplish, but by the opposition you have encountered, and the courage with which you have maintained the struggle against overwhelming odds.

*****

The road to success is dotted with many tempting parking spaces.

*****

The successful warrior is the average man, with laser-like focus.

*****

Success isn't just about what you accomplish in your life; it's about what you inspire others to do.

*****

The difference between success and failure is the ability to take the right action at the right time.

*****

Success isn't permanent, and failure isn't fatal.

*****

Success is finding something you love to do and doing it well.

*****

Success doesn't come from what you do occasionally, it comes from what you do consistently.

*****

Successful people do what unsuccessful people are not willing to do.

*****

If you want to achieve greatness, stop asking for permission.

*****

Your success will be determined by your own confidence and fortitude.

*****

Success is a state of mind. If you want success, start thinking of yourself as a success.

*****

Success is not just about making money. It's about making a difference.

*****

Success consists of going from failure to failure without loss of enthusiasm.

*****

Success is the result of preparation, hard work, and learning from failure.

*****

Success is never owned; it is only rented—and the rent is due every day.

*****

The difference between who you are and who you want to be is what you do.

*****

If you are not willing to risk the usual, you will have to settle for the ordinary.

*****

Successful people don't worry about the opinions of others. They focus on doing their best.

*****

The secret to success is to do the common things uncommonly well.

*****

Success is not in never failing, but in rising every time you fall.

*****

A successful person is one who can build a firm foundation with the bricks others have thrown at him or her.

*****

Success is not about what you have; it's about what you give.

*****

People who are successful are willing to do what unsuccessful people are not willing to do.

*****

Success is not just about the destination, but the journey as well.

*****

Success is having the courage to pursue your dreams, despite the obstacles.

*****

The successful person has the courage to make the most out of the opportunities presented.

*****

Success is when preparation meets opportunity.

*****

People who achieve success take consistent action, no matter how big or small.

*****

Success means having the courage, the determination, and the will to become the person you believe you were meant to be.

*****

The only way to achieve success is by taking action, and the only way to fail is by giving up.

*****

The successful person is the one who can handle adversity and come out stronger.

*****

When you know what you want and you want it badly enough, you'll find a way to make it happen.

*****

To succeed in life, you need two things: ignorance and confidence.

*****

Success is to live your life in such a way that the people who know you feel inspired to become better versions of themselves.

*****

Success is nothing more than a few simple disciplines, practiced every day.

*****

The first step toward success is taken when you refuse to be a captive of the environment in which you first find yourself.

*****

Success is about creating value in everything you do.

*****

The key to success is to focus on your strengths and ignore your weaknesses.

*****

Success is when you become the best version of yourself.

*****

Successful people are not afraid of failure. They learn from it and grow.

*****

The secret to success is doing what others are afraid to do.

*****

Success is the result of perfection, hard work, learning from failure, loyalty, and persistence.

*****

The only limit to your success is the amount of work you are willing to put in.

*****

Success is not about being the best, it's about doing your best.

*****

Success is not the key to happiness. Happiness is the key to success.

*****

Success is measured by how many lives you've impacted.

*****

The successful person is the one who never stops learning.

*****

Success is the progressive realization of a worthy goal or ideal.

*****

Success is not about what you have, but who you become.

*****

Success is about achieving your own personal definition of happiness.

*****

The road to success is always under construction.

*****

Success is the ability to go from one failure to another with no loss of enthusiasm.

*****

The greatest success is the ability to bounce back from failure.

*****

Your success is determined by the actions you take and the mindset you create.

*****

Success doesn't happen by accident; it is the result of careful planning and dedication.

*****

Successful people are the ones who can see opportunities where others see challenges.

*****

Success comes from what you do, not what you say you'll do.

*****

The key to success is setting goals and working tirelessly to achieve them.

*****

Success comes to those who are too busy to be looking for it.

*****

Winners are not afraid of losing. But losers are." – Robert Kiyosaki

*****

"Success is achieved and maintained by those who try and keep trying." – W. Clement Stone

*****

"Success is a state of mind. If you want success, start thinking of yourself as a success." – Joyce Brothers

*****

"Big shots are only little shots who keep shooting." – Christopher Morley

*****

"Success is nothing more than a few simple disciplines, practiced every day." - Jim Rohn

*****

"Don't let yesterday take up too much of today." - Will Rogers

*****

"The only way to do great work is to love what you do." - Steve Jobs

*****

"Success is not how high you have climbed, but how you make a positive difference to the world." - Roy T. Bennett

*****

"Work hard in silence, let your success be your noise." - Frank Ocean

*****

"The secret of getting ahead is getting started." - Mark Twain

*****

"Success is doing ordinary things extraordinarily well." - Jim Rohn

*****

"Don't count the days, make the days count." - Muhammad Ali

*****

"Limit your 'always' and your 'nevers.'" - Amy Poehler

*****

"Success is best when it's shared." - Howard Schultz

*****

"Great minds discuss ideas; average minds discuss events; small minds discuss people." - Eleanor Roosevelt

*****

"He who is not courageous enough to take risks will accomplish nothing in life." - Muhammad Ali

*****

"Be so good they can't ignore you." - Steve Martin

*****

"Perseverance is not a long race; it is many short races one after the other." - Walter Elliot

*****

"To live a creative life, we must lose our fear of being wrong." - Joseph Chilton Pearce

*****

"Success is the result of preparation, hard work, and learning from failure." - Colin Powell

*****

"I can't change the direction of the wind, but I can adjust my sails to always reach my destination." - Jimmy Dean

*****

"You don't have to be great to start, but you have to start to be great." - Zig Ziglar

*****

"Fall seven times, stand up eight." - Japanese Proverb

*****

"Ambition is the path to success. Persistence is the vehicle you arrive in." - Bill Bradley

*****

"Success is a lousy teacher. It seduces smart people into thinking they can't lose." – Bill Gates

*****

"Make each day your masterpiece." – John Wooden

*****

"Success means doing the best we can with what we have." – Zig Ziglar

*****

"If you can dream it, you can do it." – Walt Disney

*****

"The more you praise and celebrate your life, the more there is in life to celebrate." – Oprah Winfrey

*****

"Success is no accident. It is hard work, perseverance, learning, studying, sacrifice and most of all, love of what you are doing." – Pelé

*****

"Success isn't overnight. It's when every day you get a little better than the day before." – Dwayne Johnson

*****

"Success is getting what you want. Happiness is wanting what you get." – Dale Carnegie

*****

"Courage is resistance to fear, mastery of fear – not absence of fear." – Mark Twain

*****

"Success demands singleness of purpose." - Vince Lombardi

*****

"There's no secret to success. It's the result of preparation, hard work, and learning from failure." - Colin Powell

*****

"All our dreams can come true, if we have the courage to pursue them." - Walt Disney

*****

"Chase the vision, not the money, the money will end up following you." - Tony Hsieh

*****

"Success is not about being the best. It's about always getting better." - Behance

*****

"You measure the size of the accomplishment by the obstacles you had to overcome to reach your goals." - Booker T. Washington

*****

"Success comes from knowing that you did your best to become the best that you are capable of becoming." - John Wooden

*****

"Great things never came from comfort zones." - Unknown

*****

"Be fearless in the pursuit of what sets your soul on fire." - Jennifer Lee

*****

"Strive not to be a success, but rather to be of value." - Albert Einstein

*****

"You don't need to see the whole staircase, just take the first step." - Martin Luther King Jr.

*****

"Success starts with self-discipline." - Unknown

*****

"Your limitation—it's only your imagination." - Unknown

*****

"Success is a journey, not a destination." - Arthur Ashe

*****

"Nothing will work unless you do." - Maya Angelou

*****

"Opportunities multiply as they are seized." - Sun Tzu

*****

"If people are doubting how far you can go, go so far that you can't hear them anymore." - Michele Ruiz

*****

"You can't cross the sea merely by standing and staring at the water." - Rabindranath Tagore

*****

“Do not wait to strike till the iron is hot, but make it hot by striking.” - William Butler Yeats

*****

"Whether you think you can, or you think you can't - you're right."– Henry Ford

*****

"Do not wait to strike till the iron is hot, but make it hot by striking."– William Butler Yeats

*****

"I am not a product of my circumstances. I am a product of my decisions."– Stephen R. Covey

*****

"The only way to do great work is to love what you do."– Steve Jobs

*****

"Success is not final, failure is not fatal: It is the courage to continue that counts."– Winston Churchill

*****

"You miss 100% of the shots you don’t take."– Wayne Gretzky (popularized again by Michael Scott in The Office)

*****

"It always seems impossible until it’s done."– Nelson Mandela

*****

"Success is to wake up each morning and consciously decide that today will be the best day of your life." – Ken Poirot

*****

"You are what you do, not what you say you'll do." – Carl Jung

*****

"Start small, think big. Don't worry about too many things at once." – Steve Jobs

*****

"The difference between who you are and who you want to be is what you do." – Unknown

*****

Success is not how high you have climbed, but how you make a positive difference to the world.-Steve Jobs

*****

"The best way to predict the future is to create it."-Abraham Lincoln

*****

"Don't wait. The time will never be just right."-Napoleon Hill

*****

"It does not matter how slowly you go as long as you do not stop."-Confucius

*****

"Success is not the key to happiness. Happiness is the key to success. If you love what you are doing, you will be successful."-Albert Schweitzer

*****

"Believe you can and you're halfway there."-Theodore Roosevelt

*****

"Everything you can imagine is real."-Pablo Picasso

*****

"The only limit to our realization of tomorrow is our doubts of today."-Franklin D. Roosevelt

*****

William Butler Yeats

*****

"What you get by achieving your goals is not as important as what you become by achieving your goals."-Zig Ziglar

*****

"The only thing standing between you and your goal is the story you keep telling yourself as to why you can't achieve it."-Jordan Belfort

*****

"You must be the change you wish to see in the world."-Mahatma Gandhi

*****

"Success usually comes to those who are too busy to be looking for it."-Henry David Thoreau

*****

"The future belongs to those who believe in the beauty of their dreams."-Eleanor Roosevelt

*****

"Don't watch the clock; do what it does. Keep going."-Sam Levenson

*****

"Life is 10% what happens to us and 90% how we react to it."-Charles R. Swindoll

*****

"In the middle of every difficulty lies opportunity."-Albert Einstein

*****

"Everything you've ever wanted is on the other side of fear."-George Addair

*****

"The way to get started is to quit talking and begin doing."-Walt Disney

*****

"There are no shortcuts to any place worth going."-Beverly Sills

*****

"We may encounter many defeats, but we must not be defeated."-Maya Angelou

*****

"I find that the harder I work, the more luck I seem to have."-Thomas Jefferson

*****

"Success is not in what you have, but who you are."-Bo Bennett

*****

"Your time is limited, so don't waste it living someone else's life."

*****

"Strive not to be a success, but rather to be of value."

*****

"If you can dream it, you can do it."

*****

"Don't limit yourself. Many people limit themselves to what they think they can do. You can go as far as your mind lets you."-Mary Kay Ash

*****

"The best revenge is massive success."-Frank Sinatra

*****

"Be not afraid of life. Believe that life is worth living, and your belief will help create the fact."-William James

*****

"The mind is everything. What you think you become."-Buddha

*****

"Act as if what you do makes a difference. It does."

*****

"You must do the thing you think you cannot do."

*****

"Success is the sum of small efforts, repeated day in and day out."-Robert Collier

*****

"Success doesn't come from what you do occasionally, it comes from what you do consistently."Marie Forleo

*****

"Life isn't about finding yourself. Life is about creating yourself."-George Bernard Shaw

*****

"What lies behind us and what lies before us are tiny matters compared to what lies within us."-Ralph Waldo Emerson

*****

"Perseverance is not a long race; it is many short races one after the other."-Walter Elliot

*****

"Success is liking yourself, liking what you do, and liking how you do it."

*****

"Courage is grace under pressure."-Ernest Hemingway

*****

"Start where you are. Use what you have. Do what you can."-Arthur Ashe

*****

"It's never too late to be what you might have been."-George Eliot

*****

"Success is how high you bounce when you hit bottom."-George S. Patton

*****

"Don't be pushed around by the fears in your mind. Be led by the dreams in your heart."-Roy T. Bennett

*****

"Don't be afraid to give up the good to go for the great."-John D. Rockefeller

*****

"You don't have to be great to start, but you have to start to be great."

*****

"The only way to achieve the impossible is to believe it is possible."-Charles Kingsleigh, Alice in Wonderland (2010)

*****

"When everything seems to be going against you, remember that the airplane takes off against the wind, not with it."-Henry Ford

*****

"Success is a journey, not a destination."-Ben Sweetland

*****

"Opportunities don't happen, you create them."-Chris Grosser

*****

"A person who never made a mistake never tried anything new."

*****

"In order to succeed, we must first believe that we can."-Nikos Kazantzakis

*****

"The secret of getting ahead is getting started."-Mark Twain

*****

"The harder you work for something, the greater you'll feel when you achieve it."

*****

"Success is the ability to go from one failure to another with no loss of enthusiasm."

*****

"The best preparation for tomorrow is doing your best today."-H. Jackson Brown Jr.

*****

"The greatest glory in living lies not in never falling, but in rising every time we fall."

*****

"Hardships often prepare ordinary people for an extraordinary destiny."-C.S. Lewis

*****

"If you want to go fast, go alone. If you want to go far, go together."

*****

African Proverb

"Don't let yesterday take up too much of today."-Will Rogers

*****

"The only impossible journey is the one you never begin."-Tony Robbins

*****

"Success isn't just about what you accomplish in your life; it's about what you inspire others to do."

*****

"You are never too old to set another goal or to dream a new dream."

*****

"It's not whether you get knocked down, it's whether you get up."-Vince Lombardi

*****

"If you can't fly, then run. If you can't run, then walk. If you can't walk, then crawl, but whatever you do, you have to keep moving forward."-Martin Luther King Jr.

*****

"Do what you can with all you have, wherever you are."

*****

"You have to be odd to be number one."Dr. Seuss

*****

"The only person you are destined to become is the person you decide to be."

*****

"Great things never come from comfort zones."

*****

"If you're going through hell, keep going."

*****

"The harder the battle, the sweeter the victory."-Les Brown

*****

"It's not whether you get knocked down, it's whether you get up."

*****

"Be yourself; everyone else is already taken."-Oscar Wilde

*****

"Life is what happens when you're busy making other plans."-John Lennon

*****

"Do one thing every day that scares you."

*****

"Everything has beauty, but not everyone sees it."

*****

"Be the change that you wish to see in the world."

*****

"A journey of a thousand miles begins with a single step."Lao Tzu

*****

"Success is the sum of small efforts, repeated day in and

*****

"If you want to achieve greatness stop asking for permission."

*****

"You are stronger than you think."

*****

"Dream big. Start small. Act now."-Robin Sharma

*****

"Go confidently in the direction of your dreams. Live the life you have imagined."

*****

"When you have a dream, you've got to grab it and never let go."-Carol Burnett

*****

"Healing takes courage, and we all have courage, even if we have to dig a little to find it."-Tori Amos

*****

"The wound is the place where the Light enters you."-Rumi

*****

"Healing is a matter of time, but it is sometimes also a matter of opportunity."-Hippocrates

*****

"Your task is not to seek for love, but merely to seek and find all the barriers within yourself that you have built against it."

*****

"The soul always knows what to do to heal itself. The challenge is to silence the mind."-Caroline Myss

*****

"Every step taken in mindfulness brings us one step closer to healing ourselves and the planet."-Thich Nhat Hanh

*****

"You yourself, as much as anybody in the entire universe, deserve your love and affection."

*****

"To heal is to touch with love that which we previously touched with fear."-Stephen Levine

*****

"Awareness is the first step in healing."-Dean Ornish

*****

"Healing doesn't mean the damage never existed. It means the damage no longer controls our lives."-Akshay Dubey

*****

"Health is a state of body. Wellness is a state of being."-J. Stanford

*****

"Time didn't heal you. I did."

*****

God (via spiritual reflection)

"The greatest healing therapy is friendship and love."Hubert H. Humphrey

*****

"There is deep wisdom within our very flesh, if we can only come to our senses and feel it."-Elizabeth A. Behnke

*****

"Healing requires from us to stop struggling, but to enjoy life more and endure it less."-Darina Stoyanova

*****

"Spiritual healing occurs as we begin to consciously reconnect with our essential being – the wise, loving, powerful, creative entity that we are at our core."-Shakti Gawain

*****

"The practice of forgiveness is our most important contribution to the healing of the world."-Marianne Williamson

*****

"The natural healing force within each of us is the greatest force in getting well."

*****

"Healing is not linear."

*****

"Our sorrows and wounds are healed only when we touch them with compassion."

*****

"Every cell in your body is listening to your thoughts."-Deepak Chopra

*****

"Healing comes in waves and maybe today the wave hits the rocks and that's OK."-Ijeoma Umebinyuo

*****

"Your body hears everything your mind says."-Naomi Judd

*****

"When we heal the earth, we heal ourselves."-David Orr

*****

"Meditation is the soul's perspective glass."-Owen Feltham

*****

"Self-care is how you take your power back."-Lalah Delia

*****

"Caring for your body, mind, and spirit is your greatest and grandest responsibility."-Mridula Singh

*****

"Healing isn't about changing who you are; it's about changing your relationship to who you are."-Suzanne Heyn

*****

"Healing begins when we stop running and face what is."

*****

"Your illness does not define you. Your strength and courage does."

*****

"Healing is an art. It takes time, it takes practice. It takes love."-Maza Dohta

*****

"Energy flows where attention goes."

*****

"Let go of the illusion that it could have been any different."-Oprah Winfrey

*****

"There can be no transforming of darkness into light and of apathy into movement without emotion."-Carl Jung

*****

"The quieter you become, the more you can hear."-Ram Dass

*****

"Nurture your mind with great thoughts, for you will never go any higher than you think."-Benjamin Disraeli

*****

"Pain is not punishment. Healing is not reward."

*****

"What happens when people open their hearts? They get better."-Haruki Murakami

*****

"Healing is simply trying to do more of those things that bring joy and fewer of those things that bring pain."-O. Carl Simonton

*****

"You cannot heal in the same environment where you got sick."

*****

"True healing is the willingness to treat yourself and others better than the past ever did."-Matt Kahn

*****

"He who has health has hope; and he who has hope has everything."

*****

Arabian Proverb

"In the process of letting go, you will lose many things from the past, but you will find yourself."

*****

"Healing doesn't mean the pain never existed. It means the pain no longer controls your life."

*****

"Each of us has a unique part to play in the healing of the world."

*****

"You were never created to live depressed, defeated, guilty, condemned, ashamed or unworthy. You were created to be victorious."-Joel Osteen

*****

"Peace comes from within. Do not seek it without."

*****

"Don't try to calm the storm. Calm yourself, the storm will pass."

*****

"Almost everything will work again if you unplug it for a few minutes, including you."-Anne Lamott

*****

"Healing is embracing what is most feared; healing is opening what has been closed, softening what has hardened into obstruction, healing is learning to trust life."-Jeanne Achterberg

*****

"Sometimes the most important thing in a whole day is the rest we take between two deep breaths."-Etty Hillesum

*****

"To love oneself is the beginning of a lifelong romance."

*****

"I can be changed by what happens to me. But I refuse to be reduced by it."

*****

"Nature itself is the best physician."

*****

"Go within every day and find the inner strength so that the world will not blow your candle out."-Katherine Dunham

*****

"Listen to your body. It's smarter than you."

*****

"When you touch one thing with deep awareness, you touch everything."

*****

"Your body is precious. It is our vehicle for awakening. Treat it with care."

*****

"Our bodies communicate to us clearly and specifically, if we are willing to listen."

*****

"Gratitude opens the door to the power, the wisdom, the creativity of the universe."

*****

"Spiritual progress is like a detoxification."

*****

"Healing happens when you sit with the pain instead of pushing it away."

*****

"Be still, and know that I am God."-Psalm 46:10 (Bible)

*****

"An empty lantern provides no light. Self-care is the fuel that allows your light to shine brightly."

*****

"I've learned that healing is a daily choice."-Yung Pueblo

*****

"It's not selfish to love yourself, take care of yourself, and make your happiness a priority. It's necessary."-Mandy Hale

*****

"Embrace the glorious mess that you are."-Elizabeth Gilbert

*****

"True healing happens when we give ourselves permission to feel."

*****

"The soul would have no rainbow if the eyes had no tears."

*****

Native American Proverb

"One small crack does not mean you are broken, it means that you were put to the test and you didn't fall apart."

*****

Linda Poindexter

*****

"Tears are the beginning of healing."

*****

"Spirituality is not about religion, it is about connection to self and source."

*****

"Healing starts with acceptance."

*****

"The universe is not outside of you. Look inside yourself; everything that you want, you already are."

*****

"The greatest wealth is health."-Virgil

*****

"Everything in the universe is within you. Ask all from yourself."

*****

"Self-love is the source of all our other loves."-Pierre Corneille

*****

"You carry so much love in your heart. Give some to yourself."-R.Z.

*****

"Your body is your temple. Keep it pure and clean for the soul to reside in."-B.K.S. Iyengar

*****

"Nothing can dim the light which shines from within."

*****

"Breathe. Let go. And remind yourself that this very moment is the only one you know you have for sure."

*****

"Take a deep breath, and just be."

*****

"Healing doesn't mean going back to the way things were, it means finding a new way to be."

*****

"Self-care is not a luxury. It's a necessity."-Audre Lorde

*****

"Let your faith be bigger than your fear."

*****

"The body benefits from movement, and the mind benefits from stillness."-Sakyong Mipham

*****

"You don't have to control your thoughts. You just have to stop letting them control you."-Dan Millman

*****

"Let go, or be dragged."-Zen Proverb

*****

"Healing yourself is connected with healing others."
-Yoko Ono

*****

"Give yourself the same care and attention you give to others and watch yourself bloom."

*****

"As soon as healing takes place, go out and heal somebody else."

*****

"Silence is sometimes the best answer."-Dalai Lama

*****

"Balance is not something you find, it's something you create."-Jana Kingsford

*****

"You were not born to suffer."-Bentinho Massaro

*****

"Let your inner light guide your healing."

*****

"Healing begins with intention."-Chopra Center

*****

"Inner peace begins the moment you choose not to allow another person or event to control your emotions."-Pema Chödrön

*****

"Feelings are much like waves, we can't stop them from coming but we can choose which one to surf."-Jonatan Mårtensson

*****

"Take time to do what makes your soul happy."

*****

"May you transform all pain into wisdom."

*****

Leadership is not about titles, positions, or flowcharts. It is about one life influencing another. - John C. Maxwell

*****

The function of leadership is to produce more leaders, not more followers. - Ralph Nader

*****

The best way to predict the future is to create it.
- Peter Drucker

*****

Leadership is the capacity to translate vision into reality.
- Warren Bennis

*****

Do not follow where the path may lead. Go instead where there is no path and leave a trail. - Ralph Waldo Emerson

*****

Success is not final, failure is not fatal: It is the courage to continue that counts. - Winston Churchill

*****

. A leader is one who knows the way, goes the way, and shows the way. - John C. Maxwell

*****

Innovation distinguishes between a leader and a follower.
- Steve Jobs

*****

What you do has far greater impact than what you say.
- Stephen Covey

*****

Don't wait for opportunity. Create it.
- George Bernard Shaw

*****

Leadership is not about titles, positions, or flowcharts. It is about one life influencing another. - John C. Maxwell

*****

The function of leadership is to produce more leaders, not more followers. - Ralph Nader

*****

The best way to predict the future is to create it.
- Peter Drucker

*****

Leadership is the capacity to translate vision into reality.
- Warren Bennis

*****

Do not follow where the path may lead. Go instead where there is no path and leave a trail. - Ralph Waldo Emerson

*****

Success is not final, failure is not fatal: It is the courage to continue that counts. - Winston Churchill

*****

A leader is one who knows the way, goes the way, and shows the way. - John C. Maxwell

*****

Innovation distinguishes between a leader and a follower. - Steve Jobs

*****

What you do has far greater impact than what you say. - Stephen Covey

*****

Don't wait for opportunity. Create it. - George Bernard Shaw

*****